SPAIN

BY
WILLIAM ANTHONY

BookLife PUBLISHING

©2019
BookLife Publishing Ltd.
King's Lynn
Norfolk PE30 4LS

Printed in Malaysia.

A catalogue record for this book is available from the British Library.

ISBN: 978-1-78637-684-8

Written by:
William Anthony

Edited by:
John Wood

Designed by:
Gareth Liddington

Photocredits:

Cover – Abihatsira Issac, KikoStock, grop, lookus, piyaphong, DiViArt, Veja, Natasha Breen, Studio KIWI, Victoria43, 4 – Victoria43, John_Walker, Artem Kulturen, 5 – Botond Horvath, 6 – Lauramarleen, S-F, Funstock, 7 – Diego Delso, Daleen Loest, shooarts, 8 – Vicente Ortega Losa, Elizaveta Elesina, baibaz, 9 – Ana del Castillo, The_Pixel, DiViArt, New Africa, 10 – JohannesS, Natursports, Saroj Khuendee, 11 – charnsitr, Archivo personal, Yury Gulakov, 12 – TTstudio, EvgenySHCH, 13 – Paul Audouard, ismel leal pichs, 14 – Mariia Kan, grebcha, Fuel to your fire, 15 – Pajor Pawel, Bernard Gagnon, charles taylor, 16 – Melanie Lernahieu, nito, Lifestyle Graphic, Jiri Hera, 17 – Mimadeo, Visionsi, nadianb, 18 – Alvaro German Vilela, S-F, Michal.H, 19 – Tm, trabantos, patrice6000, 20 – Migel, Ana del Castillo, Victor H, nontthepcool, Ruslan Rizvanov, 21 – Iakov Filimonov, Charly Morlock, Mega Pixel, 22 – Sean Pavone, emperorcosar, njaj, 23 – Sean Pavone, Reimar, 24 – Balate Dorin, Taiga, AVN Photo Lab, Slavko Sereda, 25 – leonov.o, Victoria43, Bayanova Svetlana, kedrov, 26 – Vladimir970, Vector Plus Image, Danler, Songdech Kothmongkol, Lionger, 27 – Vitaly Titov, michael regeer, marssanya, cristi180884, 30 – Shaiith, Efired, Suti Stock Photo,

Images are courtesy of Shutterstock.com. With thanks to Getty Images, Thinkstock Photo and iStockphoto.

CONTENTS

Words that look like this can be found in the glossary on page 31.

WELCOME TO SPAIN

Hola! That means hello in Spanish. My name is Sofía. I live in Murcia in the south of Spain with my family. I still haven't seen a lot of my own country, so we're going on a road trip around Spain – I can't wait!

Look out for coordinates in boxes like these. Use the internet to explore these places online. You can ask an adult to help you.

Spain is in the continent of Europe and it has borders with Portugal and France. It also has lots of islands that aren't attached to the mainland, such as Ibiza, Gran Canaria and Tenerife.

SOME OF SPAIN'S ISLANDS HAVE VOLCANOES ON THEM, LIKE THIS ONE IN TENERIFE.

SPANISH CULTURE

My country is known for its unique culture. We are famous for our impressive dances and music, especially flamenco. We also make amazing food, such as paella!

Lots of different people live in and visit Spain. There are people from different countries, backgrounds and religions. We're going to meet so many interesting people on our journey.

I SAVED UP LOTS OF EUROS FOR OUR TRIP – THIS IS OUR CURRENCY IN SPAIN.

THE CITY OF ARTS AND SCIENCES

The first stop on our trip was Valencia to see the City of Arts and Sciences. It is a set of huge, modern buildings all based around learning about art and science.

12 TREASURES OF SPAIN

The City of Arts and Sciences is so impressive that it was named as one of the 12 Treasures of Spain. The 12 Treasures is a list of places important to the history and culture of Spain.

THERE ARE SIX MAIN AREAS IN THE CITY OF ARTS AND SCIENCES.

L'HEMISFÈRIC

One of my favourite areas was L'Hemisfèric. Inside, there is a planetarium, where you can learn about the stars and constellations in the night sky.

L'OCEANOGRÀFIC

L'Oceanogràfic was also really fun. It is the biggest aquarium in Europe. An aquarium is a place where you can see and learn about different animals that live in water.

MY FAVOURITE ANIMALS WERE THE BELUGA WHALES.

L'ALBUFERA

One of my favourite Spanish meals is paella. It is a dish that Spain is famous for around the world. It is made from rice, lots of vegetables and usually bits of seafood or meat.

THE PRAWNS ARE MY FAVOURITE BIT.

My parents brought me to L'Albufera, a lake just outside the city of Valencia. L'Albufera is the place where paella was first made.

THE SUNSET IS REALLY PRETTY OVER L'ALBUFERA.

RICE FIELDS

The rice for the local paella is grown here by L'Albufera. There are big rice fields surrounding the lake.

LA PAELLA DE MI ABUELA

My favourite paella is la paella de mi abuela, which means my grandma's paella. She makes paella using monkfish, tomatoes, prawns, mussels, peas, broad beans and the all-important paella rice. She makes it just right. I wish I could have it every day!

CAMP NOU

Football is a really big part of Spanish culture. My sister is a huge football fan, so we stopped off at Camp Nou – FC Barcelona's football stadium.

We went on a stadium tour and got to see the ground from the inside. It was enormous! My sister and I enjoyed seeing all the trophies Barcelona have won.

CAMP NOU HAS 99,354 SEATS IN IT – THAT'S ALMOST A QUARTER OF THE NUMBER OF PEOPLE WHO LIVE IN MY CITY, MURCIA. ES ENORME!

NATIONAL SPORT

Football is the most popular sport in Spain. It was introduced to us in the late 1800s and has been part of our country's identity ever since.

THE SPANISH NATIONAL FOOTBALL TEAM IN 1920

CAMP NOU
COORDINATES:
41.3809,
2.1228

EL CLÀSICO

One of our biggest rivalries is between Barcelona and Real Madrid. They are the most successful Spanish clubs and when there is a match between them it is called El Clásico.

LA SAGRADA FAMÍLIA

There's one sight that everyone needs to see while they're in Barcelona, and that's La Sagrada Família. It is one of the most famous basilicas in the world.

WE CAUGHT THE TRAM TO GET THERE. TRAMS ARE LIKE SMALL ELECTRIC TRAINS AND THEY ARE USED IN LOTS OF SPANISH CITIES.

UNFINISHED MASTERPIECE

The building of La Sagrada Família started in 1883, over 135 years ago, and it still hasn't been finished. The basilica will have 18 towers in total when the building is finally complete.

LA SAGRADA FAMÍLIA IS A ROMAN CATHOLIC PLACE OF WORSHIP. ROMAN CATHOLICISM IS THE LARGEST MAJOR RELIGION IN SPAIN.

ANTONI GAUDÍ

La Sagrada Família is one of the main works of the architect Antoni Gaudí. He worked on the basilica for 43 years. Gaudí abandoned nearly all of his other work in 1910 to focus on La Sagrada Família, until he died in 1926.

GAUDI'S WORK CAN BE FOUND ALL OVER BARCELONA.

PARK GÜELL

Before we left Barcelona, my parents took us to Park Güell, another one of Gaudí's works. It had lots of colourful buildings made using natural shapes.

SANTA MARIA DE MONTSERRAT ABBEY

On our way out of Barcelona, we travelled through Montserrat, one of the mountain ranges just outside the city. Papá doesn't like heights, so I don't think he enjoyed it too much!

STAIRWAY TO HEAVEN

DON'T LOOK DOWN, PAPÁ!

THE ABBEY

Santa Maria de Montserrat was built in 1025. People travelled from far away to trek up the mountain because it was believed that miracles were performed there.

THE ABBEY SITS AT 720 METRES ABOVE SEA LEVEL.

WHAT IS AN ABBEY?

An abbey is a building or a group of buildings where a community of monks or nuns live. Abbeys sometimes have a monastery or convent attached to them, and are led by a person called an abbot or abbess. Monasteries and convents are places where groups of religious people live and worship together.

MONTSERRAT MONKS

There are around 70 monks that live in the abbey. A monk is a male who has devoted his life to his religion and practising its teachings. Monks do not get married and usually live together in a monastery.

WE STAYED TO LISTEN TO THE CHOIR – THEY WERE AMAZING!

GUGGENHEIM MUSEUM

We had a very long drive to our next stop. We went to Bilbao in the north of Spain to see a famous contemporary art museum called the Guggenheim.

The Guggenheim Bilbao is a very odd-shaped building. It was planned by the American architect Frank Gehry. The museum is full of contemporary art, which is art made between the mid-20th century and today.

IT TOOK US OVER FIVE HOURS OF DRIVING TO GET HERE FROM MONTSERRAT.

GUGGENHEIM MUSEUM COORDINATES:
43.2693447,
-2.9336369

BASQUE COUNTRY

Bilbao is part of an area in northern Spain and south-western France called the Basque Country, or Euskadi. It is not officially a country, but it has many features of one. The first difference I noticed was that they weren't speaking Spanish there. They were speaking Basque (Euskara).

WONDERFUL FOOD

The Basque Country is known for its excellent food. We ordered some pintxos (they say it like this: peen-chos), which are small pieces of bread topped with ingredients such as cheese, figs and ham.

MY FAVOURITE PINTXO WAS THE ONE WITH PROSCIUTTO HAM AND BLUE CHEESE.

PALACIO REAL DE MADRID

THE CAPITAL CITY

I was so excited about this part of our trip! We went to Madrid to see the Palacio Real de Madrid. Madrid is the capital city of Spain and this was my first time visiting it.

THE ROYAL PALACE

MY SISTER SEEMED MOST EXCITED TO SEE THE SANTIAGO BERNABÉU STADIUM AFTER OUR TRIP TO THE CAMP NOU.

Palacio Real de Madrid, which is Spanish for the Royal Palace of Madrid, is the official residence of the Spanish royal family. They don't live in the palace any more, but they do use it for ceremonies and events.

The palace is built where an old fortress from the 9th century once stood until it burned down in 1734. King Phillip V ordered a new palace to be built in its place – the Palacio Real.

The Royal Palace of Madrid is one of the largest royal palaces in Europe. It has over 3,400 rooms and covers 135,000 square metres of floor space. We took a guided tour inside.

IT TOOK AROUND AN HOUR TO WALK THROUGH THE WHOLE PALACE - IT'S HUGE!

THE ROYAL PALACE IS DECORATED WITH BEAUTIFUL ARTWORK INSIDE.

TEATRO ROMANO DE MÉRIDA

I loved Madrid, but it was time to leave and head west. We headed to Mérida – a city in western Spain famous for its ancient ruins. I couldn't wait to learn about the history of the city.

THERE ARE LOTS OF VERY OLD BUILDINGS HERE, SUCH AS DIANA'S TEMPLE.

THE ROMANS

Mérida was founded by the ancient Romans in 25 BC. It was named as the capital of an area called Lusitania. We were able to see lots of Roman ruins on our trip through the city.

THE THEATRE

El Teatro Romano de Mérida, which means the Roman Theatre of Mérida, is the most famous ruin in the city. It was built around 15 BC to host performances for around 6,000 people.

ROMAN SHOWS

Live plays were popular with the Romans. They were performed all through the year. A local tour guide told me that, for a long time, only boys could be actors in Roman plays.

I'M GLAD THAT LOTS OF ACTORS ARE GIRLS NOW. I LOVE BEING ON STAGE!

SHOWS STILL HAPPEN HERE EVERY YEAR FOR AROUND 3,000 PEOPLE.

MEZQUITA-CATEDRAL DE CÓRDOBA

We headed back down towards the south of Spain. We travelled to Córdoba to see another religious place of worship. This building has a more complicated history than the others we visited before.

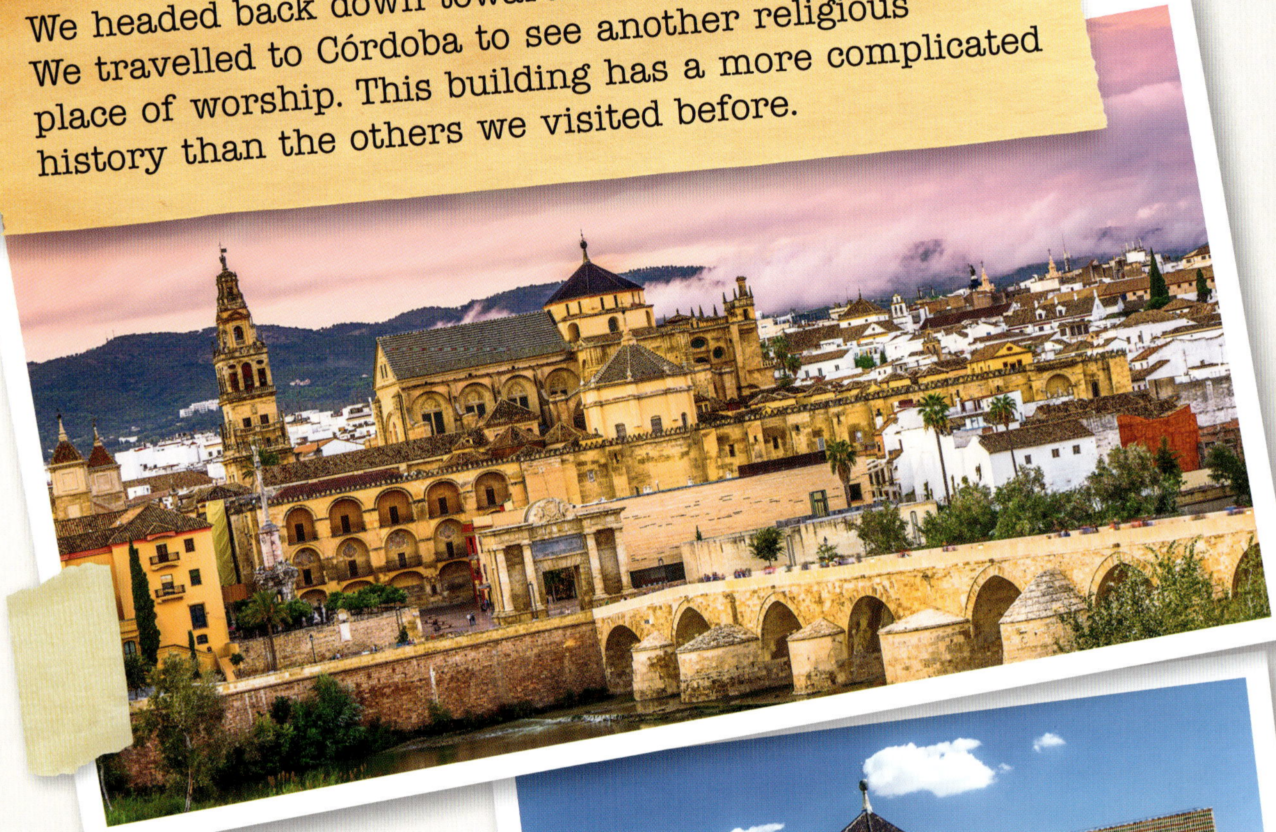

RELIGION IN SPAIN

There have been many different religions in Spain throughout history. The Mezquita-Catedral, which means Mosque-Cathedral, has been a place of worship for both Roman Catholics and Muslims since it was built.

ROMAN CATHOLICS AND MUSLIMS NEVER USED THE MOSQUE-CATHEDRAL TOGETHER.

THE MOSQUE

In AD 784, Abd ar-Rahman I bought the area of land where the Church of San Vicente stood. He ordered a mosque to be built there.

THE CATHEDRAL

In 1236, Córdoba was taken over by Christians, and they used the mosque as a cathedral. In 1523, orders were given to pull down the centre of the mosque and build a new main altar.

THE MEZQUITA - CATEDRAL DE CÓRDOBA IS ANOTHER ONE OF SPAIN'S 12 TREASURES.

GRANADA INTERNATIONAL FESTIVAL OF MUSIC AND DANCE

We're almost at the end of our trip. It's been magical so far, and I was really excited about the next part. As I said in Mérida – I love to perform on stage, and here in Granada, I got the chance!

WE'RE IN GRANADA TO TAKE PART IN THE INTERNATIONAL FESTIVAL OF MUSIC AND DANCE.

ALHAMBRA

The Granada Festival dates back to 1883, when concerts and events were held in the Palace of Carlos V and later in the grounds around the Alhambra Palace.

THE ALHAMBRA IS A MIXTURE OF A FORTRESS, A PALACE AND A CITY ALL IN ONE.

FLAMENCO

One of the most famous Spanish dances is called flamenco. The dance is known for its rhythmic footwork and sweeping arm movements. There is normally a lot of hand clapping in time with a guitar too.

FLAMENCO DANCERS CAN PERFORM ON THEIR OWN OR IN GROUPS.

TIME TO TRY

There are small shows in the festival that are made for children like me. They really inspired me when I watched them, and they let me get up to join in. <u>Me gusta bailar</u>!

THE OTHER DANCERS EVEN GAVE ME A FLAMENCO DRESS TO WEAR.

MOUNT TEIDE

Time passed so quickly on our trip – it was time for the last part of our journey. We drove to Seville airport to catch an aeroplane. We were off to Tenerife!

THE VIEW FROM THE AEROPLANE OF OUR LAST STOP

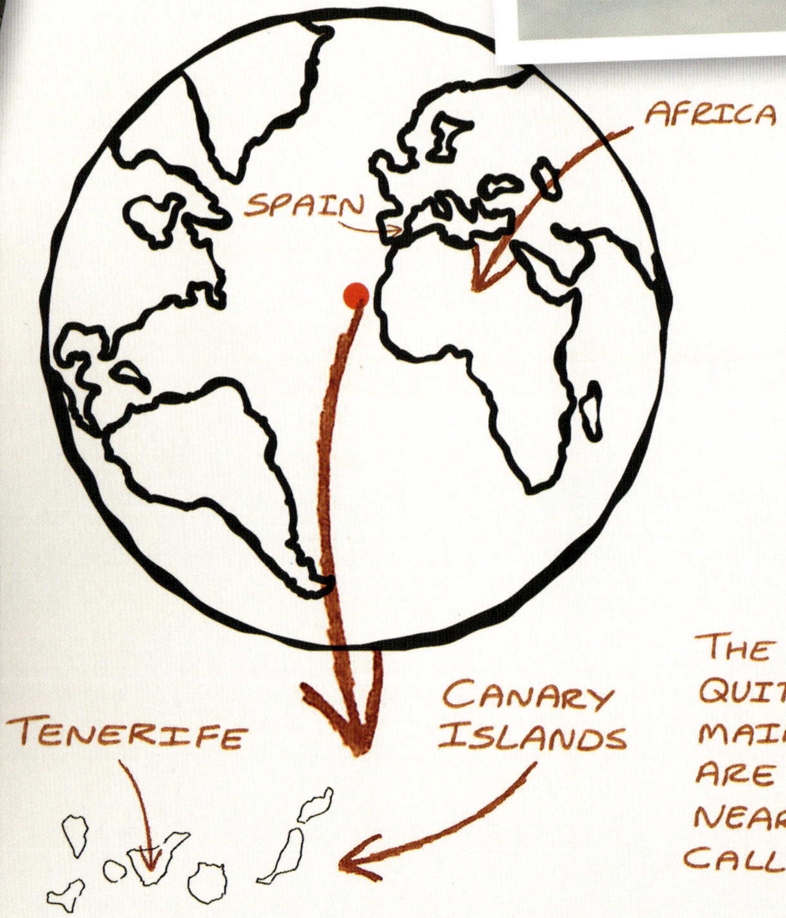

SPANISH ISLANDS

Spain isn't just the big bit of land between France and Portugal. There are lots of little islands that are part of Spain too. Tenerife is one of the Canary Islands.

THE CANARY ISLANDS ARE QUITE FAR AWAY FROM MAINLAND SPAIN. THEY ARE FOUND IN THE SEA NEAR A PART OF AFRICA CALLED MOROCCO.

THE VOLCANO

We came to Tenerife to visit the huge volcano on the island. It is called Mount Teide. We took a cable car up to the station at the top, which is 3,555 metres high.

THE TOP OF MOUNT TEIDE IS OVER 3,700 METRES HIGH, MAKING IT THE TALLEST POINT IN SPAIN.

MOUNT TEIDE COORDINATES: 28.2723, -16.6425

STARGAZING

Mount Teide has hardly any buildings on it, which means there is very little light pollution at night. Because of this, the night sky is beautiful – it is lit up by lots of stars. We ended our journey through Spain by spending the evening stargazing.

THIS WAS A PERFECT WAY TO END OUR TRIP!

THE JOURNEY

We visited so many places on our journey!

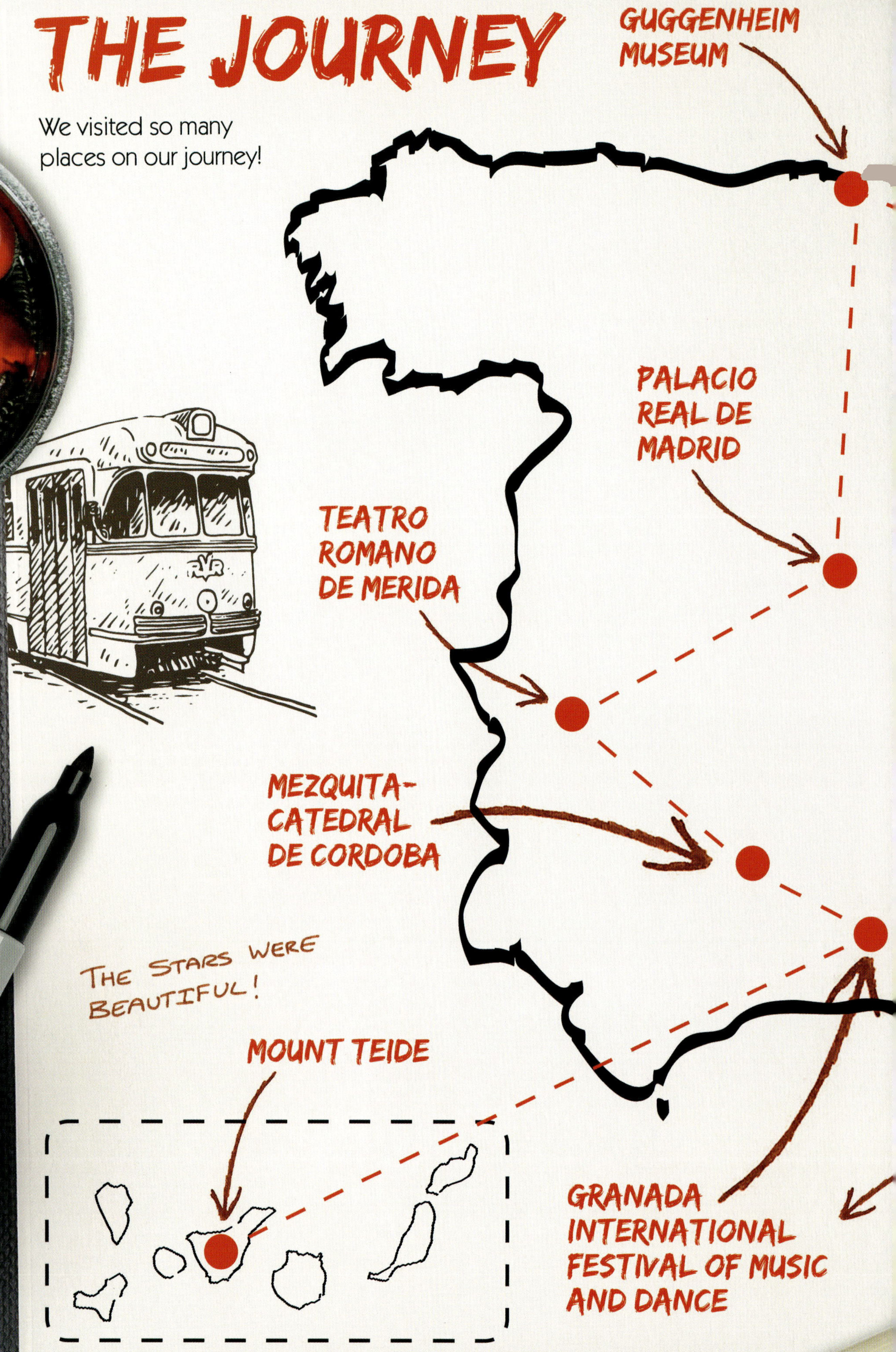

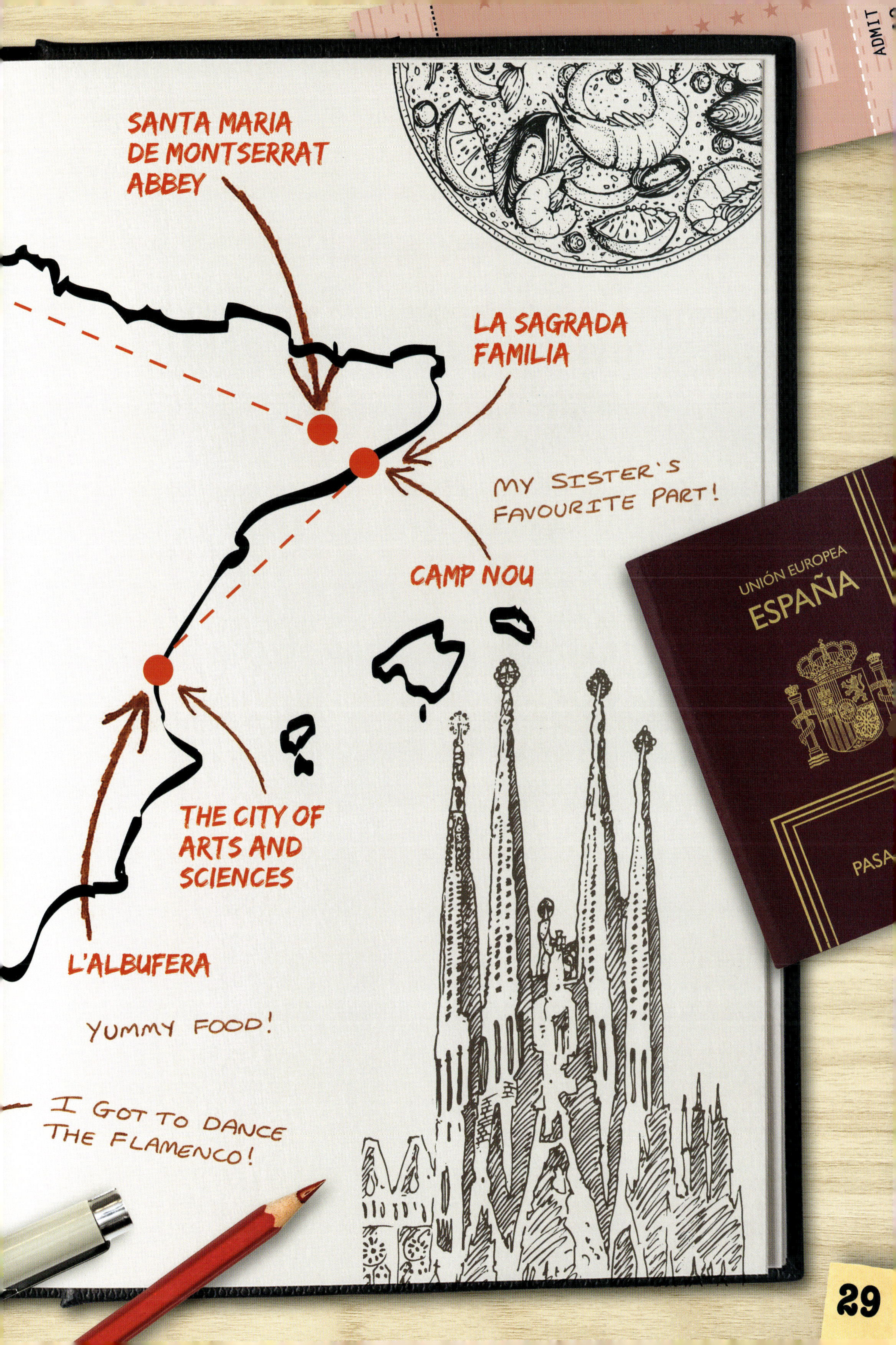
ADMIT
SANTA MARIA DE MONTSERRAT ABBEY
LA SAGRADA FAMILIA
MY SISTER'S FAVOURITE PART!
CAMP NOU
UNIÓN EUROPEA
ESPAÑA
THE CITY OF ARTS AND SCIENCES
L'ALBUFERA
YUMMY FOOD!
I GOT TO DANCE THE FLAMENCO!

ADIÓS

Adiós! We had an amazing time travelling across Spain. It was really nice to see a lot of my country that I hadn't seen before. I learned about our food, sport, art, people, history and much more!

It's hard to pick my favourite part of our journey. I loved trying out the paella in Valencia, although I also loved the Royal Palace in Madrid. But I think that the best part might have been dancing in Granada.

GLOSSARY

adiós	goodbye
architect	a person who designs buildings
basilicas	buildings that are a type of Roman Catholic church
borders	the edges of a country or object
community	a group of people who are connected by something or live in the same area
constellations	groups of stars that form a recognisable pattern or image in the sky
currency	the type of money used in a particular country
es enorme!	It is enormous!
identity	the things that make a particular person, group or place different from others
light pollution	light that makes it difficult to see things in the sky at night
mainland	a large area of land that forms a country and does not include islands
me gusta bailar!	I like to dance!
official residence	the place where someone is known to live, even if they spend a lot of time living somewhere else
place of worship	a specially designed building where people come together to practise their religion
square metres	a measurement of floor space in squares that are one metre on each side
unique	special or unusual, unlike anything else

INDEX